The Official
Baseball Hall of Fame
Story of
Jackie Robinson

JACK ROOSEVELT ROBINSON

BROOKLYN N.L. 1947 TO 1956
LEADING N.L. BATTER IN 1949. HOLDS
FIELDING MARK FOR SECOND BASEMAN
PLAYING IN 150 OR MORE GAMES WITH .992.
LED N.L. IN STOLEN BASES IN 1947 AND
1949. MOST VALUABLE PLAYER IN 1949.
LIFETIME BATTING AVERAGE .311. JOINT
RECORD HOLDER FOR MOST DOUBLE PLAYS
BY SECOND BASEMAN, 137 IN 1951.
LED SECOND BASEMEN IN DOUBLE
PLAYS 1949 - 50 - 51 - 52.

THE
OFFICIAL
BASEBALL
HALL OF FAME

S T O R Y   O F

JACKIE
ROBINSON

By Mark Alvarez

Simon and Schuster Books for Young Readers
Published by Simon & Schuster Inc., New York

A BASEBALL INK BOOK

The views expressed in this book
are solely those of the author
and do not necessarily represent
those of the Baseball Hall of Fame.

We have attempted to trace the ownership of all
copyrighted material and to secure permission from
copyright holders when required. In the event of
any question arising as to the use of any material,
we will be pleased to make the necessary corrections
in future printings. Thanks are due to the Associated
Press for the photographs on pages 72, 83, and 93; to
Les Press, Montreal, for the photograph on page 59; to
Metromedia, Los Angeles, for the photograph on page 21;
to United Press International for the photographs on
pages 9, 58, and 65; and to the National Baseball Library
in Cooperstown, New York, for all other photographs.

SIMON AND SCHUSTER
BOOKS FOR YOUNG READERS
Simon & Schuster Building
Rockefeller Center
1230 Avenue of the Americas
New York, New York 10020

SIMON AND SCHUSTER BOOKS FOR YOUNG READERS
is a trademark of Simon & Schuster Inc.
Also available in a LITTLE SIMON paperback edition.
Manufactured in the United States of America
10 9 8 7 6 5 4 3 2 1
ISBN: 0-671-69480-4   ISBN: 0-671-69093-0 (pbk.)

Contents

Jackie Robinson was a great baseball player, but his lasting fame is as a hero of American history.

◆ *1* ◆

Who Was
Jackie Robinson?

Jack Roosevelt Robinson was a great athlete.

In college, he became UCLA's first four-letter man. He starred in football, basketball, track, and baseball.

He was so good in football that some sportswriters considered him the finest running back in the nation.

In basketball, one coach called him the best player in the country.

In track, he won the NCAA broad jump title.

He was also a superb golfer, tennis player, and swimmer.

He was probably the best all-around athlete of his era. But he was much more than that. He became a symbol of freedom and strength and courage to millions of other Americans.

Jackie Robinson was the first black man in the twentieth century to play major league baseball. In 1947, he broke "the color line" that had kept fine black players out of the white big leagues and had forced them to play in the segregated Negro leagues.

It wasn't easy. There were millions of people in the

United States in those days who didn't want to see baseball integrated. And thousands of them let Jackie know how they felt. He was called horrible names. He got death threats in the mail. Some white players announced that he'd never make it in the big leagues. Others said they didn't want to play on the same field with him. There were times when he couldn't find decent housing for his family, or a place to buy lunch, or a public bathroom for his little son to use. Every time he stepped onto the field, he knew that many people were wishing him the worst and hoping he would fail. On top of that, he knew that he carried the hopes of millions of black Americans with him whenever he stepped to the plate.

Even though Jackie Robinson was a strong, tough man, all of this pressure bothered him. But he tried not to let the strain show. When other players cursed him or tried to knock him down early in his career, he refused to be drawn into a brawl, even though his first instinct was to fight back. Instead, he channeled his anger and frustration into his play on the diamond, where he was a ferocious competitor and fearsome base runner. He became one of the game's great players on one of the game's great teams—the old Brooklyn Dodgers of the late 1940s and 1950s.

As he became established in baseball, Jackie began to speak out on many issues. He said what he thought, without mincing words, so he made many people angry. He continued saying what he thought after he retired—he even wrote a newspaper column. He got involved in politics. Some of the things he said and did angered blacks and whites alike. But he continued to speak his mind and follow his conscience.

Martin Luther King, Jr., and Jackie—two champions of civil rights.

Even most of those who disagreed with him, though, still recognized that Jackie Robinson was a great American hero who had achieved an important American success. When he entered the big leagues, the integration of the game was "an experiment." After his first astonishing season, it was a fact.

When you think of Jackie Robinson, think of courage. Think of determination. Think of self-respect. Jack Roosevelt Robinson had the heart of a lion, and he inspired millions of others to their own acts of bravery. Here's his story.

◆ 2 ◆

A Tough Kid

Jackie Robinson always said, "I never had it made," and he was right. His grandfather had been a slave. His parents had toiled on a Georgia plantation. And he was born, on January 31, 1919, into an America that was a long way from giving its black citizens a fair shake.

When Jackie was only six months old, things got even tougher. His father left home and abandoned the family. Jackie never saw him again. Then, because there was no longer a man in the family to work the fields, the plantation owner threw the Robinsons—mother Mallie and five children—off his land.

Mallie Robinson had to decide what to do. How would she support her children? How would she keep the family together? How would she see to everyone's education?

She was only thirty years old, a young country woman who had never traveled far from her Georgia home. But her half-brother Burton Thomas lived in California, and Mrs. Robinson had heard enough about the West to feel that she and her four sons and one daughter would have a better chance for a good

Mack and Jackie excelled because of mother Mallie's example.

life there than they would have in the South.

It was hard to leave all her friends and relatives behind, but Mrs. Robinson was as strong and determined as her children would grow up to be. She knew what she had to do. She raised the fare by selling most of the family's possessions. Then, in the spring of 1920, she bundled all the children onto a train for the West Coast. When they left Georgia, Edgar was eleven, Frank was nine, Mack was seven, Willa Mae was five, and Jackie had turned one.

The Robinson family home in Pasadena, California.

With all those youngsters cooped up on a train for several days and nights, the trip was an exhausting one. Finally, though, the family arrived in Pasadena. At first, they lived with Uncle Burton, who didn't have much, but was generous with what he had. The house was too crowded, though, and Mrs. Robinson soon found another place to rent. Eventually, the family moved to a small house on Pasadena's Pepper Street, where Jackie and the other kids were to grow up.

Mrs. Robinson worked hard doing other people's cleaning and washing and ironing. She often got up before dawn to go to her job, and she labored long hours, but she couldn't make enough money to support her family by herself. She applied for welfare, but even with the help of the state, Mallie Robinson and her family just scraped by. They often had only two meals a day—sometimes simply bread and milk sweetened with sugar. The children were always hungry—not just a little bit, but so hungry that their stomachs hurt.

Nonetheless, the Robinson children began to grow up strong and straight. And their mother made sure they went to school. Actually, Jackie started going to Cleveland Elementary School before he was old enough to attend. With his mother working, his sister Willa Mae watched young Jackie. She took him along to school with her and left him to play in the schoolyard sandbox. He was glad when he grew old enough to start school and go inside with the other children!

California *was* a better place for the Robinson children to grow up. The schools were integrated. There were no "white only" drinking fountains or public rest rooms, and no laws that blacks had to ride at the back of public buses or ride in special train cars. But even in California, there was more than enough racial prejudice for Jackie to understand that many whites considered him a second-class citizen because of his color.

Even in California, the Pasadena city swimming pools were off-limits to blacks except one day a week. The same was true of the local YMCA. In movie theaters, blacks were expected to take seats in the balcony.

When the black community went to court and finally forced Pasadena to open its swimming pools to everyone all the time, the city's leaders got back at these "troublemakers" by firing every black worker on the city payroll. Jackie's brother Mack, who had represented his country in the Olympic Games, was one of the workers who lost their jobs.

On Pepper Street itself, many of the Robinsons' early neighbors didn't want a black family living nearby. They weren't friendly. They even tried to pay Mallie Robinson to move away. But Mrs. Robinson knew her rights. She had worked hard to find the family a decent house to live in and she wasn't about to be pressured into leaving.

Jackie was eight years old when he ran into his first violent racial problem. He was out sweeping the sidewalk in front of the Pepper Street house when a neighbor girl started shouting at him. "Nigger!" she yelled. "Nigger! Nigger!" Jackie decided to reply in kind. He'd learned from Edgar that back in Georgia the worst thing you could call a white person was "cracker." So he shouted back. "Cracker! Cracker! Cracker!" The girl's father heard him, and angrily rushed out of the

14

house. Soon, he and Jackie—a grown man and an eight-year-old boy—were throwing rocks at each other. Luckily, the girl's mother stopped the rock fight before anyone was hurt.

But there were many more fights. Jackie and his brothers didn't go out looking for trouble. Their mother would never allow that. But they didn't let racial insults go by, either.

Jackie grew up learning his rights from his mother. But he learned from the world around him that black people often had a hard time gaining their rights. And he learned from his brothers not to take any insults from anyone.

He grew up religious—Mallie Robinson saw to that. But he grew up a fighter, too.

◆

As a youngster, Jackie had a group of friends that he came to call "The Pepper Street Gang." They were mostly black or Japanese or Mexican boys, and most were as poor as the Robinsons. The Pepper Street boys hung out together, played sports together—and got into trouble together. They threw rocks at streetlights. They tossed clods of dirt at cars. And they stole—food mostly, because they were all hungry all the time, but other things as well. Captain Morgan of the Pasadena Police Youth Division knew the Pepper Street Gang well.

But the Pepper Street Gang was mostly a bunch of kids who hung out and played together. They put together teams for all the sports and challenged other neighborhood clubs. They traveled all around the Los Angeles area playing—and beating—other kids' gangs.

In the Pepper Street Gang's games, Jackie was always the best player. All the Robinsons were fine athletes, and Jackie was no exception. He seemed to be able to pick up a new sport and be terrific at it right away.

Once, he and the Gang were at a local golf course, hoping to pick up golf balls to sell back to the players. Jackie walked up to a golfer on the fairway to ask if he wanted to buy some balls.

The man said, "Double or nothing."

Jackie said, "What's double or nothing?"

The man thought he'd be able to get the balls for free. "We'll both play from here," he said. "If I get the ball in the hole in fewer strokes than you, you give me the balls for nothing. If you hole out in fewer strokes, I'll pay you double your price."

Jackie had never played golf before, but he said, "Sure."

The man handed him a putter, a club that's not meant to be used on the fairway, only on the green. But Jackie knocked the ball onto the green and holed out in fewer strokes than the man. Instead of fifty cents, his natural athletic ability had won him a dollar.

Gradually, sports became the center of Jackie's world. At John Muir Technical High School, he was a star in football, basketball, baseball, and track. And when he followed his brother Mack to Pasadena Junior College, he just kept getting better.

◆ 3 ◆

The Finest Athlete in America

Jackie had always idolized his older brother Mack. Mack was one of the fastest sprinters and longest jumpers in the world. In 1936, the tall, slender Mack won his way onto the United States Olympic team. At the Olympic Games in Berlin, he won a silver medal, finishing second to another great black athlete, Jesse Owens, in the 200 meter dash. A few weeks later, in France, he set a world record in that event. Two years later, he was national champ. At Pasadena, Mack had won virtually every event he'd competed in, and had topped it all off by setting the national junior college record in the broad jump, leaping an even 25 feet.

At Pasadena Junior College, Jackie took up where Mack had left off. He not only broke his brother's record by leaping 25 feet, 6½ inches, he also won the national junior broad jump championship. But unlike Mack, Jackie didn't specialize in track and field. He was an all-star in football, basketball, and baseball, too.

Juggling all these sports wasn't easy. Football in the fall and basketball in the winter weren't too tough, but

Jackie was an all-sports star in college, including broad jump.

in the spring Jackie really had to hustle to manage both baseball and track. He often competed in a meet and played in a game on the same day. He'd finish his events on the track and then hop into his friend Jack Gordon's car. Then he'd change into his baseball uniform as Jack sped him to the diamond where Pasadena was playing ball.

The system worked pretty well. On the same day in 1938 that he broke Mack's broad jump record at a meet in Pomona, he helped the baseball team win its conference championship in a game at Glendale.

In the spring of 1938, while he was at Pasadena Junior College, Jackie played in an exhibition game against the Chicago White Sox. He had a wonderful day, especially in the field at shortstop.

Jimmy Dykes was the White Sox manager, and his eyes almost popped out of his head when Jackie ran far to his right, snagged a grounder, whirled, and threw the batter out at first.

"Geez," whistled Dykes. "Nobody in the American League makes plays like that. If this kid was white, I'd sign him on the spot."

But, of course, Jackie *wasn't* white. And even though he knew he was good enough, it was years before he thought seriously that he might actually play for a major league team.

◆

When his two years at Pasadena were over, a host of colleges were ready to offer Jackie athletic scholarships. But he wanted to stay near his family—especially his mother and his brother Frank, who had become his greatest supporter. So he chose nearby

UCLA. The coaches there were thrilled, and so was athletic director Bill Spaulding.

"He was so good at everything," Spaulding joked later, "that I was afraid our four coaches would start fighting among themselves."

No need to worry on that score. Jackie just carried on as usual, starring in all four sports and working around scheduling conflicts as best he could. Although he was later to make his great mark in baseball, at UCLA he was most spectacular as a football player and track man.

One of his teammates on the UCLA football squad was Kenny Washington, a bruising runner who would eventually become one of the first black players in the NFL. He and Jackie complemented each other beautifully on the field. Washington powered through the line, knocking over would-be tacklers. Jackie used his speed and agility to avoid the defense entirely. This astonishing ability to change directions instantly and get up to full speed in a single stride later made him baseball's most exciting base runner. For UCLA in 1939, it meant an amazing 12.2 yards per carry and a national record of 20.1 yards per punt return.

After his great football season, Jackie went on to basketball, where he led the Pacific Coast Conference in scoring. In the spring, it was track, where he became the conference champion in the broad jump. Then he went on to the NCAA championship in Minneapolis and won there, too.

Oddly, the only sport he didn't do especially well in was baseball. With all his other sports activity, he simply didn't have time to practice enough on the diamond—and it showed. He was the Bruins' starting

In the UCLA backfield with Kenny Washington, Jackie ran over and around would-be tacklers for record gains.

shortstop, but during the 1940 season, he hit only .097 and made many errors in the field. Hardly a performance you'd expect from a future Hall of Famer.

The year 1940 was an Olympic year, and many people saw Jackie as a natural to make the United States team as a broad jumper. But World War II, which had begun in Europe in 1939, was spreading. The United States wasn't involved yet, but it became clear that there would be no Olympic Games in 1940.

But there was something even better in store for Jackie that year. One afternoon while he was working

In 1940 Jackie met Rachel Isum, the woman he later would marry.

in the student lounge, his best friend, Ray Bartlett, brought a pretty coed named Rachel Isum by to meet him.

Jackie liked Rachel right away. He felt comfortable with her and he liked the fact that she was smart as well as attractive. But at first, Rachel wasn't too sure she liked Jackie. She thought the famous athlete would be stuck up—that he would think more of himself than of anyone else.

Gradually, though, she found that she liked this handsome young man who burned with such competitive fire.

It would be years before they'd be able to marry, but Jackie and Rachel had found each other.

◆

That fall, with no Olympics in the picture, Jackie focused once again on football. He put together another superb season as a running back. And in the winter, it was another great basketball season.

But Jackie was beginning to wonder where all his athletic glory was getting him. He was spectacular on the playing field and famous all over the country for his ability as a football player and broad jumper. And yet he was still poor.

Worse, he saw no way in which his great athletic talent could help him make a good living. Today, of course, he'd be drafted by professional teams and would be able to negotiate a lucrative contract. In those days, though, the only major professional sport was baseball. And the big leagues were closed to black players.

Since Jackie saw no way to make a full-time living

as a player, he decided he wanted to do the next-best thing—work with young athletes. And he wanted to start his new career as soon as possible. He decided to leave UCLA right after the basketball season in 1941, rather than stay through the spring to graduate.

His mother didn't like this idea at all. To her, education was the key to a better life. Rachel agreed with her. And so did Mack. But Jackie had made up his mind. He was tired of being poor. He wanted to be able to help Mrs. Robinson out after all her years of working and scrimping for him and her other children. He'd gotten a good education at Pasadena Junior College and UCLA—he just wouldn't graduate. Besides, he thought, a college degree wouldn't help a black man get a job in a white man's world.

Jackie took a job with a government agency called the National Youth Administration as an assistant athletic director at one of their camps for disadvantaged kids.

Jackie thought he was starting a career as a coach and athletic director. But something beyond his control was about to change the course of his life—the entry of the United States into World War II.

◆ *4* ◆

Trouble in the Army

Jackie's job with National Youth Administration didn't last long. The government abandoned the program and closed down all the camps. Jackie wasn't sure what he should try next. But after a strong appearance in the 1941 College All-Star football game in Chicago, he was offered a chance to go to Hawaii to play semipro football with the Honolulu Bears.

This wasn't full-time football. Like the other Bears, Jackie worked for a construction company during the week and starred on the gridiron on the weekends. After the season ended, he decided to head back to the mainland to get ready for an All-Star basketball game. He thought he might turn pro, even though there was no established basketball league in those days, and the money wasn't too good.

Jackie left Hawaii on December 5, 1941. On December 7, the ship's captain told everyone aboard that the Japanese had attacked Pearl Harbor. The United States had entered the war. In a few months, Jackie, along with millions of other young men, was drafted into the Army.

Before he went into the service, though, he had

25

another chance to impress White Sox manager Jimmy Dykes during a workout in Pasadena. With a bad leg he'd injured playing football, he still ran wild on the base paths.

"I'd hate to see him on two good legs," said Dykes. "He's worth $50,000 of anybody's money. He stole everything but my infielders' gloves."

Of course, what Dykes meant was that Jackie would have been worth $50,000 if he'd been white. There were still no blacks allowed in the major or minor leagues.

◆

Soon, Jackie reported to Fort Riley, Kansas, completed his basic training, and applied for Officer Candidate School, which was known as OCS. Although he scored well on the entrance test, Jackie, like other qualified black soldiers, was not admitted to OCS.

The Army stalled for three long months. Finally, Jackie went to Joe Louis, the heavyweight boxing champion of the world, who had also been assigned to Fort Riley. Louis, the best-known and most admired black man in the country in those days, spoke to some friends in Washington, D.C. Jackie and the others were admitted to OCS.

When he graduated as Second Lieutenant Jack Roosevelt Robinson, Jackie became the morale officer of a truck battalion, in charge of keeping the men in good spirits. During World War II, the Army, like the Navy, was segregated. Black junior officers served in all-black outfits, although most higher ranks were still held by whites. In Jackie's unit, the men began to complain that the seating at the Post Exchange res-

Jackie Robinson's fight for equal rights began in the Army.

taurant was segregated, too, and that there were only a few seats assigned to blacks. As a result, black soldiers often had to wait in line to sit down, even though there were empty seats in the white section.

Lieutenant Robinson called Fort Riley's provost marshal—the officer in charge of the Military Police—and complained about the Post Exchange seating arrangements. The provost marshal, a major, said there was nothing he could do. Jackie continued to argue. The major, who assumed he was talking to another white man, finally lost his patience.

"Lieutenant," he said, "let me put it to you this way. How would you like to have your wife sitting next to a nigger?"

As he had all his life when confronted with racial insults, Jackie exploded. Over the phone, he ripped into the major, his superior officer. When he realized he'd been speaking to a black man, the major hung up. But everyone in the company headquarters, from the clerks all the way up to the colonel, heard the uproar.

Feeling that he should explain, Jackie went to the colonel, told him what had happened, and asked him to do what he could to see that black soldiers got a better break in the Post Exchange. The colonel, a white man, agreed. He wrote a letter to the general commanding the post, asking that the seating be changed—and that the provost marshal be disciplined for his racist comments.

It took a while, but the Post Exchange finally assigned more seats to black soldiers. This wasn't the solution Jackie had wanted. He thought that all seats should be open to everyone. But he was pleased that he'd at least helped improve the lot of his men—and that he'd shown them that they should protest when they were being treated unfairly.

While he was at Fort Riley, Jackie went out for the post baseball team, which was full of big leaguers and other fine players from around the country. But like the major leagues, Fort Riley's team was open to white players only. When Jackie showed up, the officer in charge told him he couldn't play.

"You have to play with the colored team," he said.

But there was no colored team. Jackie Robinson, the man who would break the color line in major league baseball and reach the Hall of Fame, was not allowed to play his country's national pastime in the United States Army.

But the Army *did* want him to play football. Jackie worked out with the team, which played not just other military posts, but major universities as well. The University of Missouri told the colonel in charge of the Fort Riley team it wouldn't play them if Robinson — or any other black man—were on the squad. Instead of standing up to Missouri, the Army dodged the problem by giving Jackie leave so he'd be away during the game. Jackie appreciated the time at home in Pasadena with Rachel and his family, but he was furious that the Army would not stand up for any soldier's right to play on base sports teams.

Jackie was getting fed up with the racism he kept running into in the Army, and he wasn't shy about saying so. From that time on, he refused to play football for Fort Riley, even though the colonel in charge threatened to order him onto the field.

"Well, sir," Jackie told him, "You can order me to play, all right. But you can't order me to play *well*."

Soon after, Jackie was transferred to Fort Hood in Texas, where he was put in charge of a platoon of the 761st Tank Battalion. The problem was that Jackie didn't know anything about tanks. He gathered his men together and told them just that. The men had been training together for a long time. They had a much better idea of what to do than Jackie did. So Lieutenant Robinson put the platoon's top sergeant in control and offered to help him any way he could.

The result was spectacular. The sergeant knew what he was doing, enjoyed giving orders, and the men worked hard for him. Before long they were the highest-rated platoon in the battalion. The colonel called Lieutenant Robinson in to praise his work with the unit, and Jackie told him how he'd put the sergeant in control. Instead of being angry, the colonel was impressed. The battalion was about to head overseas, and he asked Jackie to go along with it as morale officer.

Jackie answered that he didn't think he'd be allowed overseas, because he was still being bothered by a bone chip in his ankle from an old UCLA football injury. The colonel thought the ankle injury might be helped by hospital treatment.

One evening in July of 1944, Jackie hopped a bus from the hospital back to the post. All his friends were out on maneuvers, so he decided to head back to the hospital. At the bus stop, he met the wife of another black officer and when the bus arrived the two got on, took a seat a few rows back, and began to chat.

Suddenly the bus stopped. The driver stalked back to his two passengers and ordered Jackie to move to the back of the bus. Jackie later realized that, because his friend's wife was very light-skinned, the driver thought she was white. The idea of a black man sitting with a white woman was an explosive issue in the South in those days. Besides, black passengers were simply supposed to sit in the rear.

After delivering his message, the driver returned to the wheel, ready to drive on. But when he looked into his rearview mirror, he saw that the black man had ignored him and was still chatting with his companion.

Furious, he rushed back again. "I told you to get to the back of the bus," he shouted at Jackie, "and if you don't I'll make plenty of trouble for you."

At this, Jackie lost his temper. "I couldn't care less about you causing me trouble," he hollered. "I know what my rights are. I'm not moving out of this seat."

Jackie knew that Joe Louis and another great black boxer, Sugar Ray Robinson, had both refused to move to the backs of Southern buses. And he knew that the Army had forbidden racial discrimination on buses operating on Army posts.

At the last stop on the post, where Jackie and his friend's wife had to transfer to a city bus, the driver leaped off the bus and found his boss and some other drivers.

"There he is," he shouted, pointing at Jackie. "There's the nigger that's been giving me trouble."

Jackie walked over to the driver and shook his finger in his face.

"Look, buster," he said, "you'd better get off my back, or you're the one who's going to run into a little trouble here."

Then he and his companion turned away and started walking toward the city bus they had to catch.

Just then, a jeep full of military policemen pulled up. They were polite, and they asked Lieutenant Robinson if he would come with them and talk to their captain. Jackie thought it would be easy to get things straightened out, so he put his friend's wife on the city bus to her living quarters, and went along with the MPs. Jackie was wrong. He was in big trouble.

When he got to the captain's office, he was questioned by a civilian woman he didn't know.

"Don't you know you've got no right to sit up there in the white part of the bus?" she asked.

And then she kept snapping questions without giving Jackie time for complete answers. Finally, she complained that his responses were making no sense.

If Jackie had been what he called "a yassuh boss type," and had shuffled and said he was sorry, the incident would have blown over. But that wasn't the Jackie Robinson style. If it had been, he would have moved to the back of the bus in the first place.

Jackie didn't think the woman was the proper person to be questioning him anyway, and he was losing his patience with her. "If you'd let me finish my sentences and quit interrupting me," he said, "maybe my answers would make sense."

At this, the captain became enraged. "You uppity nigger," he shouted. "You have no right to speak that way to this lady."

Jackie was getting hot, too. "She's the one asking the questions. I have as much right to tell my story as she has to ask questions."

At this, Jackie and the captain got into a shouting match. It ended when the captain finally ordered the MPs to escort the lieutenant back to the hospital, and called ahead for him to be met by a colonel and yet more MPs. He told the colonel to expect a black officer who had been drunk and disorderly and had been trying to start a riot.

The colonel could see right away that Jackie wasn't drunk, and Jackie confirmed it.

"I've never had a drink in my life," he said.

The colonel suggested that Jackie have a blood test immediately to prove that he hadn't been drinking.

But the MP captain wasn't about to let go. He charged Lieutenant Robinson with conduct unbecoming an officer and with disrespect to a ranking officer. If Jackie were found guilty, he could be tossed out of the Army with a dishonorable discharge.

When the other black officers heard what had happened, they were as angry as Jackie was. They were also seriously concerned. If Jackie could be treated this way and then railroaded by an Army court-martial, then so could they. They wrote letters to important black newspapers around the country, especially the Pittsburgh *Courier*. The case began to attract the kind of publicity the Army didn't need. The charges against Jackie were reduced to insubordination and willful disobedience, much lighter offenses punishable only by a fine.

But Jackie felt he wasn't guilty of anything but standing up for his rights as an American and an officer in the United States Army.

His first lawyer was a Southerner who was honest enough to tell his client that he couldn't defend a black man against charges brought by a white man. He withdrew from the case. Jackie's new lawyer was from Michigan, and he jumped into the case with both feet. He made the witnesses for the prosecution look silly and he called Jackie's colonel to state that the lieutenant was a fine officer whose platoon had won the battalion's highest rating.

Jackie was acquitted. But he was disgusted with the Army, which seemed to come down on the side of the bigots and racists all too often. And the Army was pretty tired of Lieutenant Robinson, considering him "a troublemaker." For these reasons, and because his ankle injury still wasn't healed, Jackie asked for and was granted an honorable discharge late in 1944, a little less than a year before the war ended.

He was sent to Camp Breckinridge to wait for his discharge papers to be processed, and there he met another black soldier who put an idea in his head. Before the war, the man had played baseball for the Kansas City Monarchs, one of the game's best black teams. He suggested that Jackie might be able to make good money playing baseball in the Negro leagues.

A baseball career. Jackie hadn't seriously considered it before. But now he was leaving the service. He wanted to get married, and he wanted to help out his mother. These things took money, and he might be able to make a good income playing in the Negro leagues— at least for a while. Jackie began to consider the idea seriously.

◆ 5 ◆

Mr. Rickey

In 1945, Branch Rickey was the president and general manager of the Brooklyn Dodgers. He'd been in baseball all his adult life. After college, he'd caught in the big leagues, but he'd only lasted for two years. He quit and went back to law school, coaching college teams to help pay his tuition. Eventually, though, he came back to the major leagues, first as a manager, then as an executive.

Rickey had thick, bushy eyebrows and the big, gnarled hands of a former catcher. He wore bow ties, smoked a cigar, and never used a short word where a long one would do.

Once he was negotiating with a player who wanted a larger contract for the following year. Rickey leaned back in his chair, thought about the player's good performance during the past season, and allowed as how "there is a reasonable expectation of additional emolument."

The player sat there for a second, trying to figure out what Rickey was telling him, then said, "You mean more dough, Mr. Rickey?"

Despite this incident, Rickey had the reputation of

being unwilling to pay his players reasonable salaries. Sportswriter Jimmy Powers dubbed him "El Cheapo." On the other hand, his best-known nickname was "Mahatma," after the great Indian leader Mahatma Gandhi, who had been described as "a combination of God, your own father, and Tammany Hall."

Branch Rickey was not loved by all. In fact, there were many writers, players, and other baseball executives who didn't like him a bit. They thought he was pompous and greedy.

But even most of the people who disliked him agreed that Rickey was a baseball genius. He had already transformed the St. Louis Cardinals from a rotten club to one of the most successful in the game, and he was in the process of doing the same thing for Brooklyn.

With St. Louis, Rickey had created the farm system. The Cardinals became the first major league team to control a number of minor league clubs for the express purpose of developing young baseball talent. This idea seems natural to modern baseball fans, but it took Branch Rickey to come up with it.

The Cardinals under Rickey "stockpiled" young players. They signed hundreds of good young hitters, fielders, and pitchers. These boys played hard down in the minors, and the best—players like Pepper Martin, Dizzy Dean, and Joe Medwick—won their way up to the big club. The system had worked well and St. Louis had spent years at or near the top of the National League.

But other clubs had begun to catch on and build systems of their own, and even though Rickey strengthened the Dodger's farm system when he moved to Brooklyn, he knew that it wouldn't be enough

Branch Rickey was a man of genius, vision, and courage.

Before Jackie Robinson, all that kept many gifted players from a place in the major leagues was the color of their skin.

to give him the edge he was looking for.

He needed another way to get players that the other teams were missing. So he began considering seriously something he'd been thinking about for a long time— bringing black players into the major leagues.

Rickey knew that millions of black boys played ball, just like their white counterparts. He knew that thousands of young black men played serious amateur ball, usually on segregated teams around the country. He knew that hundreds of the best black players performed professionally in the Negro leagues. And he knew that dozens of these professional players were good enough to crack the major league rosters that had been all white for generations.

Branch Rickey, baseball genius, needed a new angle, a new pool of players for the Brooklyn Dodgers. He turned his eyes to the Negro leagues, where Jackie Robinson had just become the shortstop of the Kansas City Monarchs.

The Negro leagues had been around since about 1920, although there had been good black teams long before that. There were a number of Negro leagues, and none of them was as well organized as the white major leagues. Seasons ended early, teams dropped out and dropped back in, and records weren't carefully kept. In fact, many of the best black teams made most of their money barnstorming—traveling to play exhibitions against all comers—not by playing a regular schedule of games.

Baseball had been pretty thoroughly segregated from its very beginnings. The earliest baseball organization, the National Association of Base Ball Players, wrote a rule way back in 1867 "against the admission of any club which may be composed of one or more colored persons." The rule-makers wrote that letting black men play ball would lead to "some division of feeling, whereas, by excluding them no injury could result to anybody." To anybody who was white, that is.

The National Association folded a few years later, and its rule died with it. For a few years, especially in the 1880s, black ballplayers did perform for major and minor league clubs. But by the end of that decade, most had been forced out.

This happened mainly because many white players—from the North as well as the South—considered blacks "inferior." They began to complain when they had to play with them. In 1887, Cap Anson, one of the most famous players of the nineteenth century, refused to let his Chicago White Stockings take the field against a team that included George Stovey, a black pitcher.

There is an old story that Anson, a Northerner from Iowa, shouted "Get that nigger off the field!"

Whether he ever really hollered those words or not, they certainly reflected his attitude—and the attitudes of many other white players.

The great white pitcher Tony Mullane later remembered that at about the same time, Fleetwood Walker, a black man, "was the best catcher I ever worked with." But Mullane, who was known as "The Count," also said that "I disliked a Negro and whenever I had to pitch to him I used anything I wanted without looking at his signals."

Baseball didn't write a new official rule against black players, but with this sort of prejudice in the air, it didn't have to. A so-called gentlemen's agreement was

The Chicago American Giants of the Negro National League were led by Rube Foster, at the center of the back row.

enough. And by 1900, the agreement was understood—and obeyed—by everyone. The major and minor leagues—so-called Organized Baseball—were for whites only. Blacks had to form their own teams, find their own competition, and make their own way.

From the very start, there were great black players. Men like Fleet Walker, George Stovey, and the wonderful second baseman Charley Grant were followed by others like Rube Foster, who was a fine pitcher, but is best remembered as the organizer of great early teams and the Negro National League in 1920.

Over the years, star pitchers like Smokey Joe Williams and Bullet Rogan, infielders like John Henry Lloyd, Buck Leonard, Judy Johnson, and Ray Dan-

Satchel Paige was the most flamboyant star of his day. He pitched for the K.C. Monarchs when Jackie joined them in 1945.

dridge, outfielders like Oscar Charleston and Cool Papa Bell flourished in the Negro leagues, and would certainly have starred in the white majors.

White baseball people knew all about the fine black players wandering the country in buses. Dizzy Dean of the Cardinals was white baseball's most colorful character and one of the game's greatest pitchers during the 1930s. He played often in exhibition games against black teams, and he lost about as often as he won. "It's too bad those colored boys don't play in the big league," he said once, "because they sure got some great players."

White owners and managers were always telling Negro league players how good they were. Mrs. Grace Comiskey, who owned the Chicago White Sox during the 1940s, told pitcher Sug Cornelius, "Oh, if you were a white boy, what you'd be worth to my club."

But Sug was a black boy, so he was worth nothing to the Sox.

The Negro leagues did very well during the 1930s and 1940s. By the war years of the forties, even white fans knew about fastballing Satchel Paige and Josh Gibson, the slugging catcher. Everyone knew they were the equal of any players in the country. But they still couldn't show their talents in the majors. They still rode the buses from city to city, played in unlaundered uniforms, and scrambled to find decent places to sleep.

◆

This is the world Jackie Robinson entered when he agreed to play for the Kansas City Monarchs in 1945. He knew he'd be competing against the best black players in the country. He knew he would be facing some stiff competition. But he didn't realize how difficult the life would be. Despite his bad time in the Army, he simply wasn't ready for the horrors of life on the road with a black baseball team. It was, he said later, "a pretty miserable way to make a buck."

It wasn't just that the Monarchs traveled long, grinding distances in cramped buses, or that they often played on terrible fields under awful lights. It was that they all too often couldn't get decent food or find reasonable places to stay. Many hotels—and not just in the South—wouldn't accept black guests. And many restaurants wouldn't serve them. The team—like all black clubs—often wound up eating cold food on the rattling bus, and then trying to curl up in their seats for a snooze.

Most of Jackie's teammates were from the South. Many had been playing in the Negro leagues for years. They didn't like these conditions, but they were used to them. Jackie—a college boy from California—wasn't. And he didn't want to be. All summer, he was angry, frustrated, and lonely. Sometimes he got so furious at the bad treatment, and kicked up such a row, that the team had to bundle him back on the bus and drive off.

He decided that he'd quit the team, go back to California, and look for a regular job. When he told the Monarchs, they raised his pay $100 a month. He needed the money, so he stayed.

Why did the Monarchs want to hang on to this unhappy fellow? For the best reasons in the world. Despite his loneliness and anger, Jackie Robinson was one of the greatest competitors in the history of baseball. On the field, he forgot his problems and concentrated on the game. As a result, he was playing great ball, hitting about .350 and looking sharp at shortstop and on the base paths. At UCLA, Jackie had been a star in football, basketball, and track. Now, jolting around the country with the Kansas City Monarchs, he was becoming a star in baseball, too. And someone was watching.

◆

Back in Brooklyn, Branch Rickey had made up his mind to integrate the Dodgers. Along with giving the Dodgers a new, untapped reservoir of talent, he had two other reasons. First, fitting in with his image as "El Cheapo," he knew that there was a huge black population in the New York metropolitan area, and that thousands and thousands of these folks would turn out to see one of their own playing baseball in the major leagues. Just as black players were an untapped reservoir of talent, black fans were an untapped reservoir of revenue. They'd help fill the Dodgers' Ebbets Field. They'd buy hot dogs and beer and soda pop. In short, they'd help make the Dodgers—and Branch Rickey—lots of money.

The other reason was that Rickey honestly believed that no one should be barred from baseball by the color of his skin.

Way back near the turn of the century, Rickey had been the baseball coach for Ohio Wesleyan, where he'd gone to college himself. One of his players was a black youngster named Charley Thomas. Once, the team had traveled to South Bend, Indiana, for a game with Notre Dame. His took his team into a local hotel, where everything went fine until the manager refused to allow Charley Thomas to register. No blacks were allowed in the hotel.

Rickey threatened to take his whole team elsewhere unless Thomas was given a room assignment. Finally, the manager agreed to let the black player sleep on a cot in Rickey's room. Rickey remembered years later what happened that night.

"He sat on that cot and was silent for a long time. Then he began to cry, tears he couldn't hold back. His whole body shook with emotion. I sat and watched him, not knowing what to do until he began tearing at one hand with the other—just as if he were trying to scratch the skin off his hands with his fingernails. I was alarmed. I asked him what he was trying to do to himself.

"'It's my hands, Mr. Rickey. They're black. If only they were white, I'd be as good as anybody then. Wouldn't I, Mr. Rickey?'

"Charley, the day will come when they won't have to be white."

That day didn't come for a long time. Occasionally, some baseball figure would discover a terrific black ballplayer and halfheartedly try to work around the gentlemen's agreement that still existed. John Mc-Graw of the Giants, for example, once tried to introduce Charley Grant as an American Indian named "Chief Tokohoma." It didn't work.

But during the 1930s and 1940s, things began to change. Opportunities for black athletes opened up—if only a little bit. The great sprinter and long jumper Jesse Owens became a genuine American hero by winning four gold medals at the 1936 Olympic Games.

At about the same time, the appeal of heavyweight champion Joe Louis crossed racial boundaries. These men, and other great black athletes, were still discriminated against, but they were also admired by millions of whites who were forced to think about what a raw deal many of their fellow Americans faced because of their race.

With the entry of the United States into World War II—a war we fought against dictatorship and for democracy—it became ever harder to justify racial discrimination. Black leaders and journalists, along with some white liberals, were beginning to put the heat on baseball to let blacks play in the big leagues.

In 1943, Bill Veeck, who was later to introduce exploding scoreboards to baseball as the owner of the Chicago White Sox, had an idea. The Philadelphia Phillies were for sale at a very low price. Because of the war, most of the best ballplayers were in the service. The few who were still playing were scattered among the sixteen teams that then made up major league baseball. Veeck decided that he would buy the Phillies and hire the best black ballplayers who weren't in the service to play for the team. By concentrating all the best available black players on one club, he thought he could win the pennant.

Before he made the deal, though, Veeck told National League president Ford Frick what he was up to. Frick opposed the idea, and the next day, Veeck found that the Phillies had been sold to someone else.

The next year, Rickey felt that the time was right to finally break the color barrier. Kenesaw Mountain Landis, who had been commissioner of baseball for over twenty years, and who had always opposed integrating the game, had died. The war was coming to an end. Black leaders were stepping up the pressure.

Rickey called in his scouts and told them to start looking over Negro league talent. But he decided to keep his purpose a secret. He told the scouts that he was starting a new Negro league called the United States League, and that he wanted them to find talent for a team he would call the Brown Dodgers.

Very soon, his scouts began sending back reports on the heavy-hitting shortstop for the Kansas City Monarchs, a former football and basketball star who'd also been a national champion at the broad jump—an aggressive, outspoken, highly competitive twenty-six-year-old named Jackie Robinson.

◆ *6* ◆

The Meeting

When Branch Rickey's scouts went out to find the country's best black players, they looked first at a couple of the most famous. But they decided that Satchel Paige and Josh Gibson were too old. They needed to find a player who had proven that he could run, throw, and hit with power, but who hadn't already passed his best years in the Negro leagues.

The scouts looked at dozens of players, but they soon began to focus on Jackie Robinson. The more they saw of him, the more they liked him. He wasn't just proving to be a great ballplayer; he was smart and well-spoken, too. And—very important to Mr. Rickey—he came from a strong, religious family background. He neither smoked nor drank, and he acted like a gentleman.

Finally, in August 1945, Rickey sent scout Clyde Sukeforth to Chicago. Sukeforth met with Jackie and asked him to come back to Brooklyn for a talk with Rickey about joining the Brown Dodgers of the United States League.

Jackie Robinson's meeting with Branch Rickey at the Dodger offices on Montague Street became one of the most famous and dramatic in American history.

Rickey started with an odd question.

"Have you got a girl?" he asked.

Jackie didn't like this question. It was nobody's business if he had a girl or not. Besides, he wasn't sure, after his awful summer away from California, that he *did* still have a girl. Rachel didn't like the idea of his bouncing around the country playing baseball, and he hadn't seen her all summer.

"Have you got a girl?" Rickey asked again.

"Well, I don't know, Mr. Rickey," said Jackie. "I think so, but she might have lost patience with me."

"Oh, I'm sure she's still waiting for you," said Rickey. "And when we're done here today, I want you to call her up. There are times when a man needs a woman by his side."

Jackie knew then that something out of the ordinary was about to happen.

"Do you know why I asked Clyde to bring you to see me?" Rickey asked.

"Well," said Jackie, "he told me you wanted to talk to me about playing for the Brown Dodgers."

"Yes," said Rickey. "That's what he was supposed to tell you. But the truth is that you are not a candidate for the Brooklyn Brown Dodgers. I think you can play in the major leagues, and I'm interested in you as a candidate for the Brooklyn Dodgers of the National League."

Jackie couldn't speak. He knew that integration was coming, and he'd hoped, during his long summer with the Monarchs, to get a chance. But hearing the words stunned him. He sat there and stared at Rickey.

"I want to start you at our top farm team in Montreal.

Do you think you can play for them?"

Jackie was so excited and moved that he could barely blurt out a reply.

"Yes," he answered simply. He knew he could play well at Montreal. He thought he could play well *anywhere*. Like so many great black players before him, all he wanted was a chance. Unlike all the others, it looked as if he was going to get one.

Then Rickey shocked Jackie again.

"I know you're a good ballplayer, Robinson," he snapped, his bushy eyebrows bobbing up and down. "What I don't know is whether you have the guts."

"What is this?" Jackie thought. "First the guy offers me a chance to play in the big leagues, and then he insults me by questioning my courage."

Before Jackie could explode, Rickey explained what he was talking about.

"We're about to take a big step here, Robinson. A lot of people—maybe even most people—will be against us at first. We can only win if we convince the world that you are a great ballplayer *and* a fine gentleman."

"But Mr. Rickey," Jackie said, "it's the box score that really counts, isn't it?"

"That's all that *ought* to count, Robinson," said Rickey. "Maybe someday it's all that *will* count. But right now, other things count, too. The way you handle yourself. The way you react to others."

Rickey pounded on his desk. "People will call you foul names. Pitchers will throw at your head. Runners will knock you over and spike you. But if you react violently, our whole experiment might fail.

"I know you're agressive. I know you're a great competitor. I know the Army considered you a troublemaker because you stood up for your rights. That's all fine. Those traits help make you the great ballplayer you are. But if we're going to succeed in integrating baseball, you won't be able to react aggressively to taunts or even injuries. Do you think you can swallow your pride? Do you think you can control your temper?"

Jackie didn't like the way this conversation was going. He'd *never* let anyone insult or demean him without fighting back. He *believed* in retaliation. He was getting angry at Rickey. He wouldn't sell out his self-respect for anyone. Maybe this Mr. Rickey was just another white man who didn't understand that black men had personal dignity, too.

"Mr. Rickey," he snapped, "are you looking for a Negro who is afraid to fight back?"

"Robinson," Rickey exploded, "I'm looking for a ballplayer with guts enough *not* to fight back!"

Rickey leaped from his chair. "Look," he boomed, "our adversaries *want* you to react. They'll try to provoke a race riot at the ballpark to prove that Negroes shouldn't be allowed in the major leagues. They'll try to frighten the public so that they won't come to games. Our strategy has to be *not* to react. Just to play the best baseball you know how, and to act like a gentleman—even in the face of the worst taunts and foulest insults. This way, we won't just win games. We'll win friends for our cause."

Rickey knew that this would be tough for Jackie and he wanted to be sure he could control his temper. He threw off his suit jacket and charged around from behind his desk, determined to put Jackie to the test.

"All right," he growled. "I'm a hotel clerk. The hotel

only accepts whites. You come to the desk looking for a room. 'Get out of here, boy,' I say. 'We don't take niggers here.' What do you do?"

Without letting Jackie answer, Rickey acted out more scenes. He made Jackie imagine problems with racist sportswriters, with waiters in restaurants, on trains. Then he turned to the diamond.

"I'm a pitcher." Rickey wiped the sweat from his brow. "I throw at your head. What do you do?

"I'm a base runner." He bumped Jackie. "I slam into you at second base and knock you over. I scream at you. I call you nigger boy. I shove you. I tell you to get your big black butt out of my way. What do you do?

"I'm stealing second." Rickey charged Jackie and bumped him again. "I come in with my spikes high. I slice your leg open. You're bleeding. I stand up and laugh at you. 'How do you like that, nigger boy?' What do you do?"

Jackie couldn't get a word in edgewise. Rickey kept pushing him, bumping him, insulting him. He was playing the parts of all the players and fans and others who would do anything to run Jackie out of baseball. He was testing to see if Jackie could take the pressure without losing his temper.

It was hard. Jackie understood what Rickey was doing. But it still wasn't pleasant being shoved around, bumped into, shouted at, and abused.

Rickey had one more example.

"It's the World Series. I'm a base runner. I don't like your team and I don't like you. I slide hard into second base. I try to spike you, but you have the ball and you tag me right in the ribs. The umpire calls me out. I'm furious. I jump up and scream at you." Rickey went

Bound for glory—Jackie Robinson of the Montreal Royals.

toe to toe with Jackie and called him every foul name in the book. But he wasn't done yet.

"I'm so angry that I can't restrain myself. So—right out there in front of thousands of people—I punch you." Rickey swung his fist in front of Jackie's face. "I punch you right in the cheek. What do you do?"

This time Rickey waited for Jackie's answer.

Jackie knew what Rickey wanted him to say. But it was hard. Every fiber in his body told him to strike back when someone tried to intimidate him. He was proud of the fact that nobody *ever* pushed him around and got away with it. But he knew that Branch Rickey was right. He couldn't give the enemies of integration any reason for claiming black players didn't belong in baseball. He knew that it would be tough, but he knew what he had to do.

"I understand what you're saying, Mr. Rickey. He punches me in the cheek, I turn the other cheek."

"Wonderful," boomed Rickey. He pounded Jackie on the back—in a friendly way, this time. "I'm sorry I had to act that way and say all those awful things. But I had to test you. *Everything* depends on you. You can't slip even once."

Before he left Rickey's office, Jackie had agreed to play for the Montreal Royals, Brooklyn's top minor league team in the International League. It would be a tough road, but he was on his way.

◆ 7 ◆

Breaking In

After signing with the Royals, Jackie went off to Venezuela to play winter ball with a black all-star team that included his future Brooklyn teammate, catcher Roy Campanella.

But he got back in time for a major event in February of 1946: his wedding. Jackie and Rachel had been engaged for five years, waiting for the war to end, for some stability in life, for enough money to start a life together. For them, even Jackie's breaking of baseball's color barrier came second.

After their honeymoon, Jackie and Rachel headed for Florida and spring training. Almost immediately, they began running into the kinds of difficulties that Rickey had acted out.

Jackie and Rachel were bumped from planes, forced to sit in the back of buses, and were unable to find a restaurant that would serve them. They had to stay in private homes because hotels wouldn't accept them as guests. Through all of this, Jackie was furious, but he didn't let his anger show.

"I had no right to lose my temper," he wrote years later, "and jeopardize the chances of all the blacks who

Jackie and Rachel were invited into the halls of Congress but not to the nation's hotels and restaurants.

The year after Jackie reached Brooklyn, he was joined by Roy Campanella, formerly with the Baltimore Elite Giants.

would follow me if I could help break down the barriers."

Down in Florida, Rickey and his advisers already felt that Jackie was a fine hitter, a great base runner, and the best bunter in baseball. Rickey wanted to make sure that Jackie put his speed and quickness to good use.

"Give it all you've got when you run," he told his new player. "Gamble. Take a bigger lead."

This daring, aggressive style was natural to Jackie, and it soon became the Robinson hallmark as a player.

Spring training was rough. Some Florida towns

wouldn't let the Royals take the field with black players in the lineup. In Sanford, the chief of police walked right out onto the field in the middle of the game and told the Montreal manager that local laws banned black and white athletes competing together.

Jackie didn't hit well during the spring, but by the time the regular season opened in April, he had won the starting second-base job because of his speed and aggressive play.

With his very first regular season game, though, his slump at the plate ended and he showed that he belonged on the field with anyone. He started poorly.

The Royals' rookie tore up the league in 1946, hitting .349.

In his first at bat against Jersey City, he grounded out weakly to shortstop. Then he dropped the ball on a double play attempt. His error allowed both the runner and the batter to reach base safely, and also let a run score from third.

But then Jackie caught fire. The next time he came to bat, there were two Montreal runners on base. He hit a shot into the left field bleachers for a three-run homer.

In the fifth inning, he bunted for a base hit, stole second, and moved to third on an infield grounder. At third, he put on the kind of show he'd dazzle them with at Brooklyn the next year. He took his lead, bluffed a steal of home, stopped, went back toward the base, and then bluffed another steal. The Jersey City pitcher was so flustered that he stopped in the middle of his delivery to the plate. That's a balk, and it allows every base runner to move up one base. Jackie scored.

In the seventh, he singled, stole second base again, and scored on a single. In the ninth, he bunted for another base hit, moved to third on a single, danced off the base, and scored again on a balk by a confused pitcher.

In his first official game in what had been a white man's league, Jackie Robinson went four for five at the plate, stole two bases, drove in four runs, and scored four more.

On the field, Jackie's season with Montreal was a triumph. He just kept playing the way he had started against Jersey City. He led the league with a .349 batting average. He also led in runs scored, with 113. He stole 40 bases, and was the best defensive second baseman in the International League. And the other players began to notice something else about Montreal's second baseman.

"His most obvious stock in trade is his noodle," claimed New York Yankee pitcher Joe Page. "I don't think there's a smarter player in the International League."

But all season, Jackie had to put up with exactly the kind of abuse that Rickey had tried to prepare him for and that he had seen during spring training.

At the beginning of the year, some members of the Baltimore team had threatened not to take the field against Montreal as long as Jackie was in the Royals lineup.

But times had finally changed. That kind of threat had worked for years to keep black players out of organized baseball. But now, Frank Shaughnessy, president of the International League and a friend of Branch Rickey's, took a hard line. He wired the players and told them that if they carried out their threat, they'd be suspended from baseball for the rest of their lives. They played.

But the pressure remained awful. It wasn't so much the taunts of people in the stands or the bench jock-eying of other players as that Jackie had to hold all of his anger inside. He couldn't fight back the way he had all his life. He couldn't let his real feelings out. So the tension mounted inside him.

Even when he wasn't playing in front of hostile crowds, Jackie always felt as if he were carrying the weight of his whole race around on his back. He felt that he *had* to make good so that millions of other black Americans would have chances, too.

Under all this pressure, Jackie began having trouble

sleeping. He couldn't eat a whole meal. Rachel was so worried that he might be approaching a nervous breakdown that she made him see a doctor. The doctor told him to take a rest, so Jackie did—for one day. Then he got right back into the lineup. He was leading the league in batting, and he was worried that if he rested any longer, he'd be accused of sitting out to protect his average.

Montreal finished the 1946 season in first place in the International League. In the Little World Series against American Association champs Louisville, the Royals dropped two of the first three games at Louisville, where angry white fans were all over Jackie—and his teammates.

"Hey, black boy," one of them yelled, "go on back to Canada—and stay"

"Yeah," shouted another. "And take all your nigger-loving friends with you."

The insults never let up, and for once, they got to Jackie. He couldn't concentrate, and he went one for eleven during the three games.

But things changed back in Montreal. The Royals' fans came out in droves to support their team, and to give the Louisville players a little rough treatment of their own. Montreal won three straight to win the series.

After the last game, Montreal fans stormed the field, grabbed Jackie and paraded him around the field on their shoulders. He finally had to break away and run down the street to escape the adoring crowd. Sportswriter Sam Mason wrote that "it was probably the only day in history that a black man ran from a white mob with love instead of lynching on its mind."

Soon after the season ended, Jackie and Rachel became parents. Jackie Robinson, Jr., was born in November, the first of three Robinson children who were to come along over the next few years.

◆

For spring training in 1947, Branch Rickey arranged for both the Dodgers and the Royals to train in Havana, Cuba. He thought that by doing this he could avoid some of the racial incidents that would inevitably have cropped up in Florida.

Jackie was disappointed to be assigned to the minor league Royals again instead of the big league Dodgers. He was also stunned to be told to learn to play first base—a position he had never played before. But the Dodgers had Eddie Stanky—probably the best in the National League—at second base. They needed help at first, though, and Jackie realized this might be his quickest route to the majors.

A few other Dodgers thought so, too, and they didn't like the idea. They decided they would sign and circulate a petition stating that they would not play on the same team with a black man. They hoped to keep Jackie off the Dodger roster.

Rickey got wind of the plot, though, and squashed it quickly. He called in each player individually, told him that no petition would make him change his plan, and said that any man who wouldn't play on the same team with Jackie might as well quit right then. The petition drive collapsed.

But Rickey was worried about how people—both inside and outside baseball—would react when he brought Jackie up to the Dodgers. He was afraid there would be violent demonstrations and all sorts of other trouble. He finally decided that it would be easier for many people to accept a black man in the major leagues if he was signed as the result of great pressure from his future teammates or from local fans. So he came up with a plan.

The Royals and the Dodgers would play a number of exhibition games against each other in Havana. Rickey told Jackie, "I want you to be a whirling demon against the Dodgers. "I want you to concentrate, to hit that ball, to get on base by any means necessary. I want you to run wild, to steal the pants off them, to be the most conspicuous player on the field—but conspicuous only because of the kind of baseball you're playing."

Rickey was hoping that if Jackie played well, the Dodger players would see how much he could help the team in the coming season, and ask for him to be promoted to the major league squad. He also hoped that the Brooklyn and New York sportswriters covering the team would write articles that would create a demand for Jackie among the fans back home.

Jackie did exactly what was asked of him. In seven games against the Dodgers, he hit .625 and stole seven bases.

But the Brooklyn squad still wasn't about to request the promotion of a black player.

So Rickey tried another plan. He asked the Dodgers' manager, Leo Durocher, to tell the sportswriters that Brooklyn needed Robinson at first base if they were going to win the pennant in 1947.

Before Durocher could act, though, he was banned from baseball for the season as the result of a feud with

Commissioner Happy Chandler. Chandler accused Durocher of associating with undesirable characters.

Rickey was furious. He thought the ban was unjust, but he was also worried that the bad publicity would really hurt the Dodgers. He quickly realized, though, that announcing the signing of a black player to a major league contract was such big news that it would push the Durocher scandal right off the front page. He immediately signed Jackie to a Brooklyn Dodger contract.

Jackie signs up for 1949—not as newsworthy a contract as his first, which rocked baseball to its foundation.

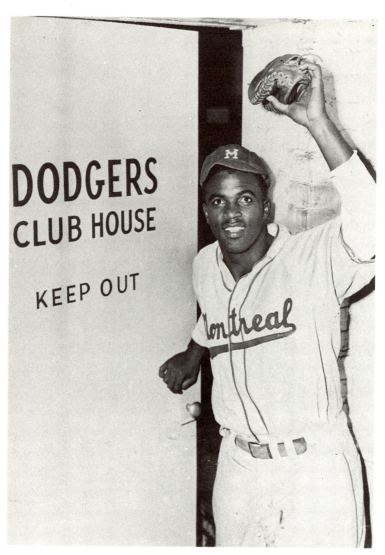

Other doors would open to black players, on other major-league teams. But Jackie was the one who opened all the doors.

Rickey was right. The Robinson story was the biggest of the year. This wasn't the most glorious way to get to the big leagues, but Jackie had made it. He was the first black man in the twentieth century to become a major league baseball player.

Everybody—not just baseball fans—began to focus on this young black man. People realized that this was not just a baseball story. Breaking the color barrier in America's national pastime was important because it reminded people of all the other barriers that would have to be broken—and it showed people that these barriers *could* be torn down. Jackie Robinson, a twenty-eight-year-old rookie baseball player, became a hero to people who'd never seen a baseball game.

But Jackie's troubles were by no means over. In many ways, they'd just started. Rickey might have signed him, millions might have come to admire him, but many others hadn't accepted him.

Early in April, the Philadelphia Phillies came to Brooklyn. Their manager was an Alabaman named Ben Chapman, and Chapman encouraged his club to harass Jackie with the foulest kind of abuse yelled from the Phillie dugout.

In baseball, "riding" opposing players by shouting insults at them was common. The idea was to get an opposing player so worked up over what he was hearing that he couldn't concentrate on the game. Everybody in baseball was used to this "bench jockeying" and considered it a part of the game.

But the things that Chapman and his Phillies shouted at Jackie upset even baseball people.

"Hey, nigger, why don't you go back to the cotton fields where you belong."

"They're waiting for you in the jungles, black boy."

They shouted that Jackie smelled bad. They yelled that he should be back home cleaning toilets. They sneered that if he were white he'd still be in the minor leagues.

The Phillies never let up through the whole series at Ebbets Field. It was so bad that other Dodgers got fed up, too.

Eddie Stanky, who was, like Chapman, from Alabama, walked over to the Philadelphia dugout and shouted, "Listen, you yellow-bellied cowards! Why don't you yell at somebody who can answer back?"

Even Dixie Walker, who had been one of the ringleaders of the petition plot, told his friend Chapman that he should lay off.

Jackie himself made believe that the abuse didn't bother him. As he'd agreed with Branch Rickey, he didn't react. But he was boiling inside.

"I have to admit that this day, of all the unpleasant days of my life, brought me nearer to cracking up than I have ever been," he wrote years later. "For one wild and rage-crazed minute I thought, 'To hell with Mr. Rickey's "noble experiment."' I thought what a cleansing thing it would be to let go."

More than anything else, Jackie wanted to charge the Phillies dugout and get his hands on the men who were calling him such vile names. But he didn't. He kept the long-term goal in mind. He kept control of himself.

Commissioner Chandler heard about what was going on during the Dodgers-Phillies series. He reprimanded Chapman and instructed the Phillies to tone it down. But Chandler couldn't control the reactions of people outside baseball. Jackie got death threats in the mail. Goons claimed they were planning to kidnap Jackie Jr. Rachel was threatened. A Philadelphia hotel refused to put him up.

Just a few weeks after his trouble with the Phillies, Jackie watched another team hit the headlines with anti-Robinson plans. Some members of the world-champion St. Louis Cardinals had talked about pulling a strike rather than playing against the Dodgers with Jackie in the lineup.

A New York sportswriter heard about the plan, contacted Ford Frick, the president of the National League, and then wrote a story about the situation.

In his article, the writer quoted Frick as warning the Cardinals, "If you do this you will be suspended from the league. This is the United States of America, and one citizen has as much right to play as another. The National League will go right down the line with Robinson."

This kind of public backing helped Jackie stay on an even keel under the tremendous pressure. But next to Rachel's steady love and support, the greatest help came from the Dodgers' captain, shortstop Pee Wee Reese. Reese was from Kentucky, and he'd grown up sharing the standard prejudices against blacks. But he was a decent, thoughtful man— one of the most respected players in the league. He felt that Jackie had a right to play ball just like anyone else.

One day during pregame warmups in Boston, the Braves (who played there before they moved first to Milwaukee and then to Atlanta) were heckling Reese brutally for being a Southerner yet playing with a black man. Pee Wee didn't answer by shouting back. He

Pee Wee Reese eased Jackie's acceptance by players and fans.

demonstrated his answer. He left his position, walked over to first base, and put his arm around Jackie's shoulder. He was showing the world, "This is my teammate. This is my friend. Color doesn't matter. We stick together." Reese became Jackie's closest friend on the Dodgers.

As the 1947 season went on, the pressure on Jackie never let up. As Rickey had predicted, runners tried to knock him down or spike him. Middle infielders kicked him or stepped on his legs after he'd slid into second base. Furious bigots kept sending obscene and threatening letters. And the verbal abuse, both from the stands and from the dugouts, was constant.

Jackie hated all this. And he hated not being able to holler back or return a shove. But he kept his anger and frustration inside. All he did on the field was play ball.

And did he play!

He hit .297, scored 125 runs, and led the league with 29 stolen bases. His intensity, his quickness, and his ability to rattle pitchers with his darting moves on the bases impressed baseball people and excited fans.

Jackie brought thousands of fans into ballparks all over the league. Many black men and women attended games just to see the amazing and wonderful sight of a black ballplayer on a major league diamond. Many others—black and white alike—came to see Jackie's fast, aggressive, heads-up style of play.

His fine season won him the Rookie of the Year award. In those days the award wasn't broken down by league, so the voters were saying that Jackie was the best new player in *both* major leagues, not just the National. (Forty years later, baseball commissioner

Bill "Bojangles" Robinson hands the keys to Jackie on his Day.

Peter Ueberroth announced that the Rookie of the Year award would be called "The Jackie Robinson Award.")

His wonderful play also helped the Dodgers win their first pennant in six years. Even though the club lost the World Series to the powerful New York Yankees, it had been a great year for Brooklyn. In a way, it had been a great year for America.

Just before the regular season ended, the Dodgers hosted a Jackie Robinson Day at Ebbets Field. His fans showered him with gifts— everything from a television set to a new Cadillac.

The Brooklyn club had brought Mallie Robinson from California for the event, and after it was over, she approached Branch Rickey to thank him for all he'd done for her son.

"Don't thank me, Mrs. Robinson," Rickey told the woman who had labored hard her whole life to raise her five fine children. "I have to thank you. If it had not been for you, there wouldn't be any Jackie."

◆ 8 ◆

The Brooklyn Years

After his fine, pressure-packed rookie season, Jackie became a mainstay on a Brooklyn club that developed into one of the greatest teams of all time. From 1947 through 1956—the years Jackie played in Brooklyn—the Dodgers won six National League pennants. And in two of the four years they didn't take the top spot, they lost out on the very last day of the season.

The year 1948, though, was a disappointment. Jackie reported overweight from all the banquets he'd attended in the off-season, and the Dodgers never really put things together. Rickey had traded Eddie Stanky to Boston, and he led the Braves to the pennant. Brooklyn, with Jackie taking over at second base, finished third.

But 1949 was something else. There were two other black players on the team by then. Catcher Roy Campanella was short and round, but he was also on his way to three Most Valuable Player awards and election to the Baseball Hall of Fame.

Don Newcombe was a tall, powerful pitcher who would rack up a few honors of his own—Rookie of the

The Most Valuable Player of 1949 greets homer-hitting Roy Campanella, the MVP of 1951, '53, and '55.

Year in 1949 and later both an MVP and a Cy Young Award as baseball's best hurler.

Rickey and Robinson's "great experiment" had proven a success, but there was still bitterness against black players in the big leagues. Many teams still weren't eager to add them to their rosters, and it would be decades before the first blacks became coaches, managers, or executives. But the arrival of great players like Campanella and Newcombe left no doubt that black ballplayers were in the major leagues to stay.

Because of this, Jackie felt that he no longer had to hold his temper and turn the other cheek when he was insulted or challenged. Rickey agreed. In 1949, Jackie would be Jackie. If pitchers threw at his head, he challenged them to fight. If opposing players shouted insults from the dugout, he insulted them back.

He began to argue with umpires, too. In fact, he started arguing so often and so heatedly that he became the toughest man in the league for umpires to deal with. Once, to let an umpire know that he didn't like a call, Jackie went back to the dugout and wrapped a towel around his throat to show that he thought the ump had "choked" on a close play. This was a common baseball gesture, but Jackie was tossed out of the game and fined.

Many fans and baseball people didn't like these new developments. They preferred the quiet, turn-the-other-cheek Robinson. But this was the real Jackie: angry, assertive, aggressive, competitive— and argumentative.

Freed from the terrible pressure of holding in his emotions, Jackie played the best ball of his life. He batted over .300 for the first of six straight years, and his .342 won the batting title. His 37 stolen bases led the league, too. And he drove in 124 runs. He had such a great season that he was named the National League's Most Valuable Player. And he led the Dodgers into the World Series again.

At the age of thirty, Jackie was in his prime, and he looked every inch the great athlete he was. He had broad "football" shoulders and the odd, rolling, pigeon-toed, almost dainty walk shared by many sprinters. His combination of bulk, strength, speed, and pure aggressiveness made him an infielder's nightmare when he came charging down the base paths. And even when the ball beat him to the base, he was often quick enough to avoid the tag with a skillful slide.

When he was in the field himself, Jackie set defensive records for second basemen.

As a batter, Jackie never hit more than 19 home runs in a season. But his hard line drives often seemed to come just when Brooklyn needed them. In a lineup filled with sluggers like Campanella, Duke Snider, and Gil Hodges, it was Jackie who batted fourth—in the "cleanup" spot reserved for the man most likely to drive in runs with men on base.

"Jackie could beat you every way there was to beat you," said Roy Campanella years later. "I have never seen a ballplayer that could do all the things that Jackie Robinson did."

And Campanella wasn't just talking about Jackie's physical skills—he was talking about his mind, too.

"He could think so much faster than anybody I ever played with or against," said Roy. "He was two steps and one thought ahead of anyone else."

People who saw him play were amazed over and over

again by his effect on a game. It wasn't just his hitting or his fielding or even his daring base running. It was his attitude, his desire, his aggressive drive to win that showed up in every aspect of his game. As he had at Montreal, he rattled pitchers into balking him along, and he tricked outfielders into throwing to the wrong base behind him.

During the late 1940s and early 1950s, Jackie was one of the finest all-around players and the biggest drawing card in the league.

The Dodgers fell just short of the National League pennant in both 1950 and 1951. Both times, the race didn't just come down to the last game—it came down to the last inning.

In 1950, a tenth-inning Dick Sisler home run won the pennant for the "Whiz Kids" of the Philadelphia Phillies.

And in 1951, Bobby Thomson of the New York Giants hit the most famous home run in baseball history— "the homer heard 'round the world"—to beat the Dodgers in the last game of a three-game playoff for the pennant.

Jackie had had terrific seasons in both those years, but he would gladly have traded his individual success for a Dodger pennant.

He was one of the most famous men in the country by this time. Millions loved him—and millions loved to hate him. He wrote newspaper articles. He appeared on radio shows. He even made a movie, playing himself in *The Jackie Robinson Story.* He made more money from endorsements and other activities off the diamond than he did directly from baseball.

Many of Jackie's teammates were famous, too. The

Jackie moved from first base because of this man, Gil Hodges.

Preacher Roe was a Brooklyn mound ace, going 22–3 in 1951.

Dodgers were especially strong "up the middle." Roy Campanella was the best catcher in the league. Pee Wee Reese and Jackie at shortstop and second base turned double plays as well as anyone in baseball. And in center field, the great Duke Snider could do it all: the Duke was a wonderful defensive outfielder with a gun for an arm—and he also hit 40 or more home runs five years in a row during the mid-1950s.

At first base, Gil Hodges was a strong and graceful presence who seemed to be able to snag anything thrown in his general direction. And, like most of the Dodgers, he could hit. Between 1949 and 1955, he never knocked in fewer than a hundred runs.

Over at third, Billy Cox regularly performed magic. Decades later, many people who saw him play still think he was the best defensive third baseman ever.

And in right field, Carl Furillo was solid, consistent, and productive. He was called "The Reading Rifle" because he came from that Pennsylvania city and his arm was so strong. Furillo was less spectacular than many of the other Dodgers, but he always seemed to bat around .300 and to knock in 90 or so runs. In 1953, he was good enough to lead the league in hitting, with a glittering .344 average.

Dodger pitching during this era was wonderful, too. Don Newcombe, Preacher Roe, Joe Black, Carl Erskine, and later Clem Labine and Johnny Podres made the Brooklyn staff as solid as any in the league.

Because they had all this talent, the last-minute losses of 1950 and 1951 were especially heartbreaking. But the Dodgers—and their fans—didn't lose heart. They came back to win in 1952 and 1953. For all their skills, though, they still could not shake the Yankee jinx: New York beat them in the World Series in both years, as they had in 1941, 1947, and 1949. The Dodgers were frustrated, and their fans were beginning to get tired of hearing the old advice: "Wait till next year."

Finally, in 1955, Brooklyn put it all together. They won the pennant by 13½ games, then they beat the Yankees in an exciting seven-game World Series. The Dodgers were champions of the world!

Jackie joined the celebration as happily as anyone. Winning the Series with the Dodgers was one of the greatest thrills of his life. But he knew that his career was nearing its end.

Back in 1953, a young second baseman had come up from Montreal. Jim Gilliam was a great prospect. In fact, he was *so* good that he took Jackie's position. Jackie became a sort of utility man *de luxe*. He played left field. He played third base. He played wherever he was needed. And he had another great year.

Gilliam had a wonderful season, too. He was named Rookie of the Year in the National League. In a way, this was a triumph for Jackie, as well as for Jim. From the time Jackie had broken the color barrier and won his own Rookie of the Year Award in 1947, six of the seven National League winners, including Gilliam, had been black players. Jackie knew better than most people that baseball—and America — had a long way to go before achieving true racial equality, but he could also see that his battles had accomplished something, not just for himself, but for others, too.

It was more of the same in 1954. Jackie had another fine season, mostly in the outfield and at third base, even though the Giants, led by the great Willie Mays,

In baseball's most daring type of play, Jackie steals home
in a 1948 game at Pittsburgh's Forbes Field.

beat the Dodgers out for the pennant.

By 1955, though, Jackie could feel that he wasn't
playing as well as he had. He was thirty-six—old age
for a ballplayer—and his hair was even beginning to
turn white. He was gaining weight and slowing down.
Some reporters were even calling him "the old gray fat
man."

But during the '55 Series he demonstrated that the
magic wasn't gone yet. In the first game, with Jackie
on third and the Yankees leading 6–4, Whitey Ford
decided to take a full windup, rather than pitch from
the stretch to hold Jackie close to the base.

Jackie had always considered it an insult when pitchers didn't take him seriously enough to watch him carefully. As Ford began his windup, Jackie took off for the plate. In came the pitch. Down went Jackie into a hard, driving slide. Yankee catcher Yogi Berra grabbed the ball and dove toward Jackie's legs to put on the tag. Behind the cloud of dust, the home plate umpire's hands went out. Safe! Jackie had stolen home in the World Series! Not bad for an old gray fat man!

The next year, Jackie helped the Dodgers to yet another pennant— their last in Brooklyn. Unfortunately for the Dodgers, the Yankees recovered from

Brooklyn's greatest team, and its only World's Champions.

Rachel and son David pose with Jackie just after news broke of his trade to the rival New York Giants.

their defeat in 1955 and came back to win the 1956 Series.

Jackie knew it was time to leave the game. He had been looking for good opportunities outside baseball for several years and he was about to come to an agreement with Chock Full O' Nuts, a New York restaurant chain.

Before he could sign his contract with Chock Full O' Nuts, though, he was shocked to learn that the Dodgers had sold him to the New York Giants.

When the Giants learned Jackie was planning to retire, they offered him $60,000 to play one more year.

This was a huge salary in those days. Jackie thought things over, but decided that it was really time to quit baseball and get on to another career. Besides, he didn't want people to think that he had threatened retirement only to squeeze even more money out of the Giants, as Dodger general Manager Buzzy Bavasi had announced to the press.

Jackie Robinson was thirty-seven years old when he left baseball. He'd played in the major leagues for ten years. He'd suffered unimaginable pressure. To millions, he'd been a hero. He'd been one of the great players of his era. Now it was time to do something else.

◆ 9 ◆

After Baseball

Long before Jackie left baseball, he'd thought about managing a team, or even moving up the ladder to become a club executive. Jackie was smart, he was articulate, and he was a proven leader of men. Despite his hot temper, he had exactly the attributes owners look for in a manager. He'd discussed the idea with Branch Rickey, who had told him he'd consider it when Jackie's playing days were over—especially if Jackie would go back to UCLA and finish up the last few months of requirements for his college degree.

But his chance of becoming baseball's first black manager ended when Rickey left Brooklyn after the 1950 season. Rickey had been forced to sell out by Walter O'Malley, who eventually moved the team to Los Angeles in 1958.

Jackie and O'Malley didn't get along. Like a lot of sportswriters and baseball people, O'Malley liked Jackie when he was quietly doing his job during his first two years in the majors. But he didn't like the real Jackie—the tougher, more outspoken man who appeared when he and Rickey agreed he didn't have to turn the other cheek.

One day in the spring of 1952, O'Malley had called Jackie into his office in Florida and asked him to bring Rachel along. He said that Jackie had disappointed fans because he'd missed an exhibition game. He also said that he couldn't understand why Jackie was complaining about staying in a segregated hotel during spring training. After all, Jackie and Rachel had been putting up with segregated living arrangements in Florida since 1946.

Jackie thought that O'Malley was being unfair on both counts. He angrily explained that he hadn't played in the game because he'd been injured.

Then he told O'Malley that he thought the Dodgers should be fighting for the rights of all their players to stay in whatever hotels they wanted.

"If you think I'm going to put up with the same conditions I had to tolerate in the past," he told O'Malley, "you're dead wrong. It doesn't strike me as fair to have people who are sitting in comfort in an air-conditioned hotel lecture me about not complaining."

O'Malley didn't agree. He called Jackie a crybaby for sitting out the game with an injury. Then he called him a prima donna—somebody who expects special treatment—for complaining about the segregated hotel.

This infuriated Jackie, but it made Rachel even angrier. She leaped in to defend her husband.

"I've seen him play with sore legs, a sore back, and sore arms," she said. "He does it because he thinks about his team. Nobody worries more about this club than Jackie Robinson, and that includes the owners."

Rachel knew that O'Malley didn't like Branch Rickey. He'd even told people in the Dodger offices not to mention Rickey's name. And she understood that

Because Walter O'Malley (above) disliked Branch Rickey, Jackie had no prospect of a management post with the Dodgers.

one reason O'Malley didn't like Jackie was that Jackie made no bones about being Rickey's friend. Rachel knew that Jackie and Branch Rickey had had their differences, but she also knew that Rickey would never have accused Jackie of lying about an injury or of being a troublemaker because he was standing up for his rights.

"Bringing up Jackie into organized baseball was not the greatest thing Mr. Rickey did for him," she told O'Malley. "Having brought Jack in, he stuck by him. If there was something wrong, he would go to Jack and ask him about it. He would talk to Jack and they would get to the heart of it like men with a mutual respect for the abilities and feelings of each other."

Faced with *two* furious Robinsons, O'Malley dropped his lecture. But he never tried to understand Jackie, or to deal with him as Rickey had. And because he controlled the team, Jackie would never get a chance to manage or move up as an executive.

◆

Much of Jackie's life after baseball was as stormy as his life on the field.

Even when he'd still been playing, he'd spoken up on a whole variety of issues. In 1953, for example, he'd said on the radio that he thought the New York Yankees discriminated against black players.

Jackie thought he was stating the obvious. The Yankees were, after all, the only New York team with no blacks on the roster. But his statement caused an uproar. He received another flood of hate mail. Sportswriters around the country weren't used to ballplayers discussing anything but what happened on the field, and many of them labeled Jackie a "soap box orator," a "rabble rouser," or worse.

To the very end of his life, Jackie Robinson was at the center of similar controversies. This happened because he always said what *he* thought—not what someone else *wanted* him to think.

He battled with figures in the white world when he saw that men in power were ignoring or oppressing his people. And he battled with leaders in the black world when he felt they were heading down the wrong path.

Here, Jackie's induction speech at the Baseball Hall of Fame.

Typically, he never mouthed the "party line"— of any party.

◆

In 1962, the first time his name appeared on the ballot, Jackie was elected to the Baseball Hall of Fame. Just as he'd been the first black man in this century to play major league baseball, he was also the first black man elected to the Hall. But he wasn't elected because he was black. He was elected because he was a great player. Here's what his plaque says:

JACK ROOSEVELT ROBINSON
Brooklyn N.L. 1947 to 1956

Leading N.L. batter in 1949. Holds fielding mark for second basemen in 150 or more games with .992. Led N.L. in stolen bases in 1947 and 1949. Most Valuable Player in 1949. Lifetime batting average .311. Joint record holder for most double plays by second baseman, 137 in 1951. Led second basemen in double plays 1949–50–51–52.

During the 1960s, the Robinson children were growing up. Sharon had been born in 1950, and David had come along in 1952. Jackie Jr., the oldest, joined the Army in 1964 and was sent to Vietnam, where he was wounded. But when he returned from the war in 1967, he came back addicted to drugs. He entered a rehabilitation program. After much anguish and agony, he beat his dependence on drugs. Jackie Jr. became drug-free. He even became a counselor at Daytop, where he'd been rehabilitated. And he began talking to groups of youngsters, telling them about the dangers of drugs and the horrors of addiction.

Jackie Jr. had been "clean" for over three years when he was killed in a car crash in June of 1971. He'd been driving back to the Robinson house in Connecticut from New York, where he'd been arranging for musicians to play at a benefit to raise money for Daytop.

His death was a terrible tragedy for Jackie and

Rachel. "You don't know what it's like to lose a son, find him, and lose him again," Jackie wrote soon after. He and Rachel could never get over their cruel loss, but they took great comfort in Sharon and David.

Jackie himself had been sick for a long time. He'd developed diabetes during his thirties, and as he got older, it began taking a greater and greater toll on him. By the early 1970s it had badly affected his sight.

In October of 1972, Jackie was interviewed on national television just before a World Series game between the Cincinnati Reds and the Oakland A's.

"I'd like to live to see a black manager," he said, frankly.

Only nine days before his death, Jackie stood beside Commissioner Bowie Kuhn at the 1972 World Series.

Jackie Robinson had the courage to remain silent, and the
nerve to speak out, as duty to his cause demanded.

As usual, there was an outcry. Why had Jackie said such a "negative" thing about baseball during the Series? Didn't he know better than to use an event like the World Series as a platform for his "political" statements? But Jackie thought he had an obligation—a duty— to speak out. He'd integrated the game almost twenty-five years before, but the first black manager had yet to take his place in a dugout. Jackie was losing patience with the owners and executives who ran the game, so he said what he thought.

As a friend of his later said, "What better place? What better time?"

He would have been saddened but not surprised to hear his old teammate Al Campanis say on TV fifteen years later that there weren't many blacks in baseball management because they didn't have "the necessities" to handle such jobs. Jackie knew that even well-meaning people like Campanis carried prejudices around without knowing it.

◆

A few days after the 1972 controversy, Jackie collapsed and died. He was only fifty-three years old, but he was sick and worn out.

"A life is not important," Jackie wrote shortly before he died, "except in the impact it has on other lives."

Yes, Jackie Robinson was the first black man to play big league baseball in this century. Yes, he was a Hall of Famer. Yes, he was one of the finest all-around athletes of the century.

But he was more than all of those things.

He set an example of personal dignity and self-respect. He was a constant spokesman for the downtrodden. He was a living symbol of strength and courage and determination. He considered, even during the horrible pressures of breaking baseball's color barrier, the effect his actions would have on the success of other black men and women who were trying to break through barriers of their own.

Jack Roosevelt Robinson. An important life? What do *you* think?